Ars longa, vīta brevis est.

©2022 Emily Silversmith · North Landing Books · All rights reserved

The beautiful sea life illustrations in this collection come from Victorian-era books on zoology, from the reports of explorers, and from academic journals documenting marine species around the world. I have gone through thousands and thousands of original pages, selecting only illustrations that depict sea creatures and plants with both realism and artistic skill. I made sure every image is clear and sharp. I digitally isolated each one from its original background, placed it on white, and color-corrected to restore the original look.

I use vintage illustrations for decoupage. If you layer multiple illustrations in your decoupage work, you have to cut them out. Therefore most illustrations I have selected are relatively simple in their outline and can be cut out without loss.

Besides decoupage, you can use these images for school projects, scrapbooking, junk journaling, and greeting card making. You can also collage them for many genres of mixed media art.

I hope you enjoy my book! Happy crafting, beautiful one!

Emily Silversmith

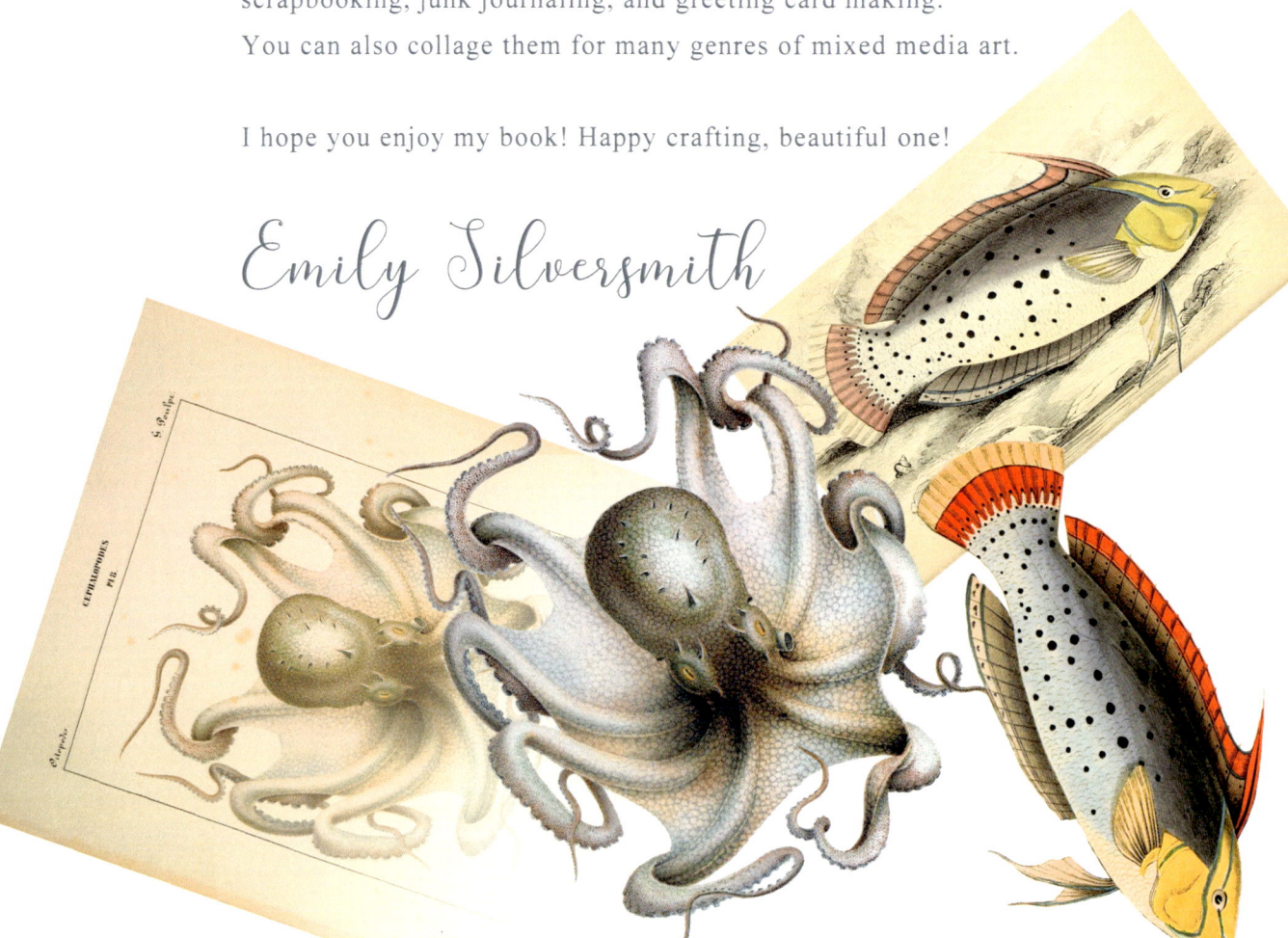

LE POULPE COLOSSAL.

www.ingramcontent.com/pod-product-compliance
Lightning Source LLC
LaVergne TN
LVRC091354060526
838201LV00042B/416